A Lifetime in a Day

SAMUEL L. GREGORY JR.

PAGE PUBLISHING, INC.
Conneaut Lake, PA

First originally published by Page Publishing 2020

ISBN 978-1-64701-327-1 (pbk)
ISBN 978-1-64701-328-8 (digital)

Printed in the United States of America

A Lifetime in a Day

In the morning, we are born to a wintry world so cold,
As the noon brings forth the spring, childhood takes on a mold.
Summer leads to midday, young adults soon grow old,
Thrust into a fall night, of age our story is told.

SELF

Each time you read this book of mine,
Something different you shall find.
You'll scan closely from cover to cover,
The intensity of self shall you discover.
Each time you glance, you'll find something new,
And there, you'll focus for a second or two.
But the main theme that will linger in your head
Are things you've forgotten or left unsaid.

Good Morning

Dew in the flowers,
Sky divided by light.
Light that's illuminating,
But not very bright.
Chirping of birds,
Natures alarm clock.
The key to the day,
Activity to unlock.
A deep breathy sigh,
To shift gears of the heart.
Touching cold earth,
The only place to start,
Staggering wearily
To be revitalized.
Outwardly moving
With inward sighs,
Rejuvenating rituals
Of opening eyes.
The future awaits,
Destiny cries.

WINTER

Brisk winds blowing to and fro.
Forecast calling for below zero.
Naked trees stand firm and brittle.
Normal activities are reduced to little.
A covering of ice stands on the ponds.
A carpet of white envelopes the lawns.
Chimneys spew breath into the air.
Light reflecting on white, a picture so rare.
Various impressions left on the ground.
Silent paths speaking, yet nothing found.
Extreme warmth only found inside.
Till this all passes, here I'll abide.

BIRTH

It's pretty dark in here. I wonder if I'll ever get out. Seems I've been in here forever.

There has got to be more to life than this. Now and then I hear sounds, but I don't know what they are. My food supply seems to be holding up exceptionally well. I think I'll kick around a bit, maybe I'll be noticed. Hey! Wait a minute, I sense an opening. This must be the way out; nope, not quite large enough. Maybe if I kick around a little more, I can expand the opening.

Uhhhh!

What was that? Something pushed me, or did it pull me? Hmm, seems to be some type of suction.

Uhhhhh!

There it goes again. Gee! That's going to be hard to fight. Let's see what I can hold onto.

I don't seem to be able to find anything.

Uhhhhhh!

There it goes again. What could it be, and what are these noises I hear?

Uhhhhhh! Uhhhhhh!

Wow! It seems this force is getting stronger and happening much more often.

Something above me is beating at a very rapid pace. It sounds like someone is anxious to get a message out on a drum.

Uhhhhhhhh! Uhhhhhhhhh!

The opening is now very easy to see. I better get out of here before something happens to me.

Uhhhhhhhhhh! Uhhhhhhhhhh!

Hey, let go of my head. It hurts!

Uh! Uh! Uh! Uh! Uh!

Ohhhhh!

This is such a tight squeeze, but I must make it out.

Ahhhhhhhhhhhhhhhhhhhhhhhh!

Goodness gracious, what a force. Finally, I'm out. Now, wh…wh…wait a minute?

Why are you turning me upside down?

All the blood is rushing to my head!

SMACK.

Wahhhhhhhhh! Wahhhhhhhhh!

That hurt! "I want to go back." "Put me down."

Wahhhhhhhh!

Wait a minute!

I recognize the sound of this individual, but I haven't seen her in this light.

I think I'll call her…

Mom.

INNOCENCE

A couple steps, then I fall.
I get back up, I feel tall.
A few teeth in front, none behind.
A small space that I call mine.
Faces around, I love to smile.
This notation I'll make in my file.
When I sense danger, I sound an alarm.
To ward off strangers, hurt or harm.
Everything I see, I must feel.
Is it a dream, is it real?
My shoes are tight, my feelings torn.
I've learned so much since I've been born.

GENTLE BREEZE

Sky so blue, clouds so pure,
How much beauty can one endure?
A drop of rain, a beautiful flower,
What more need be seen in an hour?
Take your time, relax awhile,
Enjoy life and learn to smile.
Make your days full of laughter,
Grasp the dreams that you've been after.
Don't just see the sky as blue,
Look at the infinity it offers you.
A beautiful silk sheet that goes on and on,
That is ever present from dusk till dawn.
Now and then, it's not so mild,
Sometimes, it's covered by a massive cloud.
A mask of darkness in shades of gray,
Moving and shadowing all in the way.
This is only temporary, don't get depressed,
Those rolling masses soon shall rest.
Out of nowhere, a bright cloud shall form,
Offering reflections of light so warm.
The beams of beauty will be seen from afar,
As if the glorious light of the North Star.
Just by knowing this wonder is above
Gives you the feeling of reaffirmed love.
Open your eyes and relax your mind,
And many new miracles of old you shall find.
Possibly a stone, perhaps a flower,
Or maybe even a day long hour.

CHILDHOOD

My skin is soft.
My hair like silk.
My eyes are curious.
My mind is like a computer being programmed.
All that surrounds me controls my future.
Life to me is having fun.
When I'm punished, I cry out as if life has ended all at once.
Grass is green, the sun is yellow, flowers are beautiful.
Trees are tall, seems I'll never reach the top.
People are friendly; they all appear to be good,
Except the strangers I'm told who want to hurt me.
Ugly is fighting between those who are much larger in size, or
a bitter argument amongst those close to me.
As a sapling, I grow to reach my height.

OVERSHADOWED

A reflection of someone,
Movements uncontrolled.
Trickle-down theory,
I watch my life unfold.
Very similar features,
Movements quite the same.
Have I an identity?
I know I have a name.
To break from the pattern,
I go against the flow.
I try hard to avoid
The route I'm pulled to go.
I do things unique,
To try to break the trend.
It seems of another,
All my moves depend.
I have to be different,
I want to be just me.
Possibly someone can help,
Or show me how to be.

BOUNDARYLESS

Undaunted grace shifting to and fro,
No definite task but a need to know.
Suspended, motionless, high above the ground,
A picture of perfection totally unbound.
Each shift of the wind brings forth a drift,
An air pocket is a drop, a swoop is a lift.
Effortlessly soaring in a huge sea of blue,
Infinite area and ever-changing hues.
A span of excellence, an eye to the ground,
An overview of everything that might be unsound.
Suspended by faith, exercised through will,
Upwardly reaching with the utmost of zeal.
An exercise of power, a test of might,
What better challenge than a higher height!

REALIZATION

What is right? What is wrong?
Questions that have been asked for oh so long.
Who is to say where the line is drawn?
Majority rules and the decisions gone.
I've only learned what I've been taught,
And what I've picked up, which seems a lot.
In all, I do I feel damned,
Because within, I've been programmed.
Why was this allowed to be?
Why can I not choose to be as I see?
How can one truly be blessed
Without using one's discretion in one's success?
Who makes the limits? No one can say.
So I guess I'll keep struggling in another one's way.

EDUCATION

As a giant sponge we travel about,
Seeking what knowledge we can out.
A constant thirst more to devour,
Not even realizing we're increasing in power.
Taking all in and hiding it away,
Storing for use at the right time of day.
All that is abounding, we bring inside,
We squeeze some out and some we hide.
The more we get, the more we desire,
Like adding gasoline to a burning fire.
We take it all in until we're full,
And from our vast storage, we begin to pull.
At our peak of saturation, we begin to seep,
Now others nearby, on these muscles, can leap.

INVISIBLE THOUGHTS

Why should one think obscene?
Is your purpose in life to be mean?
Try to avoid an idle mind,
Occupy your extra time.
Shun the feelings that are not civil,
Put behind your thoughts of evil.
Can you see society building?
You have to feel the hate unyielding.
Is it necessary to keep the beat?
Cross out all thoughts of open deceit.
Take away my eyes, I still despise.
Take away my ears, I still have fears.
But take away my longing soul,
And you've taken away my every goal.
My soul, something you can't see or touch,
But nothing else could mean so much.
It is the difference in life and death,
The span of time that I have breath.
Be it taken, then I am lost,
It's not worth it at any cost.

BELOW ZERO

Social separations as flurries abound,
Silently, but thoroughly disguising the ground.
Divided by class, like ice on a stream,
A glacier forms and becomes the theme.
Run off from the glacier becomes the trail,
Slippery footholds, the wintry jail.
Wind chills of religion blow into play,
Impairing vision along the way.
Sleet as racism calls out for cover,
Yet sun shining to point out another.
Feelings as barren trees toughen and age,
Becoming use to the pattern, acceptance of rage.
Fires ablaze to add warmth to the trend,
Unfortunately, not outside, only within.

NOONDAY

A break in the day, a time set aside,
A time to relax, a place to hide.
All stress put on hold, all task defied,
A perfect opportunity for your mind to decide.
Backward, forward, side to side,
In only self can you truly confide.
Allow yourself to dream as you see,
Make a plan to set yourself free.
Put up your feet, let yourself relax,
Enjoy the hour and yourself, don't tax.
Be productive in self-direction,
For your own welfare have self-affection.
Keep your eyes open, don't you slumber,
Should you become another number.

SPRING

Buds forming rapidly,
Genes flowing fluently.
Flowers opening briskly,
Colors speaking loudly.
Scents abounding thickly,
Thorns becoming prickly.
Awareness forming rapidly,
Thoughts flowing fluently.
Ideas opening briskly,
Opinions speaking loudly.
Sense abounding thickly,
Thorns becoming prickly.

JUDGMENT

Down trodden by opinions,
Whipped to tears,
Reopening wounds,
Enforcing fears,
Inflicting pain,
Causing decay,
Victoriously standing
Alone in some way.
Roaring proudly,
Approaching the throne,
A decision is reached,
The seed is sown.

DEVASTATION

Love
Sharing
Happy
Harmony
Peace
Hurt
Confused
Distraught
Anger
Festering
Hatred
Planning
Devastation

LUCKY STRIKE

This feeling in me so deep down inside
Seems to be broiling, it will no longer hide.
It's soon to come out, but how soon, when?
Will it just keep sparking again and again?
If yet it should come out, I sure can't say,
Perhaps it's the feeling that this is my day.

PEERLESS

I reign in my own world.
I answer to no one.
I make my own decisions.
I carve my own path.
I have set myself a direction.
I am a good person.
I do right by others.
I am the master of my destination.
I know what moves to make.
I live mainly for me.
I have no true boundaries.
I'm a go-getter.
I'm a chance taker.
I have the answers.
Just ask me a question.

Awareness

Walking
Talking
Feeling
Seeing
Perceiving
Understanding
Alert
Aware
Traveling
Persuading
Touching
Focusing
Thinking
Sorting
Eager
Knowing

OF AGE

A spirit of freedom,
Curiosity to address
A total sum
of eager zest.
Expanding outward
In a lunging quest,
One foot forward,
new grounds to test.
Stepping out boldly
un-tread ground.
Free to decide,
no longer bound.
Situations surface,
Freedom to choose.
A roll of the dice,
a win or a loose.
Such a great feeling,
freedom of choice.
I'm now grown,
Now hear my voice.

LOOKING DOWN THE BARREL

Looking down the barrel,
A shell to ignite.
Adjusting my aim,
My prey is in sight.
Closer and closer,
my prey to my range.
Is this the right weapon?
Small thoughts I exchange.
Squeezing the trigger,
I see my prey fall.
To my fellow hunters,
I let out a call.
Moving in briskly,
I see the eyes of my prey.
A lifeless corpse
Before me doth lay.
The absence of breath,
Animation denied.
At my hands a death,
I feel it inside.
I see myself
standing down range,
Banish that thought,
Wow! That was strange.

REFLECTIONS OF SELF

Looking straight forward,
I see a mess.
A menace to man,
I must confess.
Pushing in my way,
What I believe.
Facing others who don't
want to receive.
I have ideas that
I must share.
No set of ears
shall I spare.
I see a picture
Looking at me,
I'm trapped by myself,
I need to be free.

THE WIND BLEW

When I was a child and the wind blew!
Everything was so simple in my view.
My friends and I stuck together like glue,
When I was a child and the wind blew.

When I was a child and the wind blew!
The grass in the morning would be filled with dew.
Water and skies were shades of blue,
When I was a child and the wind blew.

When I was a child and the wind blew!
I'd see a rainbow in its infinite hues.
I'd watch as things around me grew,
When I was a child and the wind blew.

When I was a child and the wind blew!
Seemed I never ran out of things to do.
Every day I dreamed of something new,
When I was a child and the wind blew.

The wind blew! And
The wind blew! And
The wind blew.

Summertime

Green
Blue
Yellow
Red
Hot
Fun
Water
Sweat
Drink
Eat
Shade
Games
Friends
Light
Fishing
Camping
Green
Blue
Yellow
Red
Refreshing
Plenteous
Happy
Smiles
Laughter
Wet

Infinite
Porch
Swing
Hammock
Green
Blue
Yellow
Red
SUMMER.

SUCCESS

To be successful, you must make a set route,
Follow one path without jumping about.
Although many obstacles may stand in your way,
Keep on pushing, don't delay.
Lengthen your stride, stand your ground,
If you are swayed, your goal won't be found.
Overcome these problems bit by bit,
By using your knowledge, common sense, and wit.
The only thing you may never surpass
Is the assumed feeling of self-destroying crass.
Clear your mind, never say can't,
It will become your ongoing chant.
Instead, say "I can," and believe it's true,
Before you realize, you'll see a way through.
Lengthen your stride, stand your ground,
If you are swayed, your goal won't be found.

FEAR

The present unknown that threatens harm,
Keeps ever alert that inner alarm.
Halting us from reaching our goals,
By playing havoc within our souls.
By being held back, we're totally subdued,
As a normal feeling, fear soon is viewed.
Enough rope doth fear allow,
As we grow wiser, fear raises a brow.
Although we feel quite comfy within,
Fear yet abides as if a friend.
Outwardly searching should something hide,
Yet unaware fear lives inside.
With shaky hands and pacing feet,
We've found an enemy we must defeat.
The very first step in becoming aware
Is befriending fear, if you dare?

MIDDAY

Dashing through life, unconcerned about time,
constantly struggling for life sublime.

Though a battle of chaos roars in my mind,
Still peace and tranquility I seem to find.

So many things I have yet to say,
Though many activities dictate my day.

I must grab hold and secure some ground,
But before I can reach, I must be unbound.

I have a new invention everyone can try,
A brand-new vision for the longing eye.

Though it's not written down, I know what it is,
When I'm able to share it, I'll be called a whiz.

Just wait till you see what I have to share,
So many ideas no one can compare.

I could elaborate and, on my thought, expand,
Unfortunately, my hourglass is about out of sand.

THE VOICE OF THE LORD

As a fresh scented breeze blowing in the spring,
As lovely as the bells that noonday brings.
A subtle calmness like a picture perfect pond,
A ray of beauty like the coming of the dawn.
As wonderful as a feather floating on the air,
Drifting to and fro, without worry or care.
Feeling blush all over as if to be admired,
Going forth with direction, infinitely inspired.
Floating throughout the airways where eagles once had soared,
What else could this be than the voice of the Lord.

FOCUS

If you want something out of life,
Material things or even a wife.
Stand up straight and make a command,
Steady your feet and clinch your hand.
Make known to the world you've staked your claim,
And you'll take no less than this which you aim.
Believe in it as if it were law,
And not just an illusion that you may have saw.
Don't lose track of this thing that you want,
It's not even necessary to search or hunt.
Now, when this set effort comes around,
Whatever you do, don't turn it down.
One is looked up to who stands firm,
and doesn't waver throughout the term.

Till Death Do Us Part

Do you marry for sex or just plain love,
Or is it something else you're thinking of?
Do you really want to become husbands and wives,
And is this the true someone we want in our lives?
Can you smile from thick to thin,
Yet still feel love way deep within?
Can you feel angry and rot gut mad,
Yet still bear the smile that you once had?
When your mate falters and tells you the facts,
Can you still love, will your thoughts relax?
When you get old and you're future endowed,
Will you still mean the things which you once vowed?
When your mate passes, will you cry honestly "Oh, honey,"
Or will your thoughts dwell on all that money?

"WHY?" CRIED THE BRIDE

On such a day as this, with all this wedding bliss,
A moment sought by all, the day the plight must fall.
As tension fills the air, one last longing stare,
Quickened by the bells, the train leaves silent trails.
Now, words fill the air, precious metals very rare,
As the veil reveals a face, a kiss begins the race.
A kiss begins the race, cried the bride sullen face.
Such a rapid pace, have I more of life to taste?
Standing alone, I reach inside, a world of wonder no one to confide.
Are there any adventures that I haven't tried?
Is this a mark in my selfish pride?
When asked to wed, could I have lied because
the pressure that was applied?
As I look my groom eye to eye,
I now understand why a bride would cry.

MARRIED TO ME

What would it be like to be married to me?
Lord, I'd have to compare to my relationship to thee.
Not enough hours in a day to read,
Too much to do to fall on my knees.
My wants I won't sacrifice; I'll get what I see.
I'll come home to you when I have a need.

Lord, what would it be like to be married to thee?
I'd have to compare with your relationship to me.
Exalted above the angels is where I would be.
You would fulfill my each and every need.
No good thing would you withhold from me.
My eyes would be open to my ministry.

What would it be like to be married to me?
As I follow God wherever he leads?
Honoring him in the highest degree,
Being open to the anointing that ministers to me.
Such a wonderful marriage this could be.
Keeping Christ as the focus, that is the key.

TOGETHERNESS

The tears of sorrow, the pain of laughter,
We two will share in the lone hereafter.
All secrets and our sacred dreams
Will blend together, like threads to seams.
Our minds shall join in intercourse,
An in-eruptible shield to any force.
We'll blend harmoniously throughout the years,
Sheltering and destructing what could be fears.
When we conquer our dreams in life,
As one we'll stand, husband and wife.
Never looking backward, always ahead,
The peaks we've reached are grounds we've tread.
Upward, onward, to our adjoined domain,
All obstacles are knowledge we'll ever retain.

HOME

Home is a place where, no matter what we do, we are still accepted.
A place where we may be whatever we wish to be.
We may act the way we wish to act and
say the things we want to say,
It is the only place we are accepted fully,
although we may have flaws.
Why is it that we stay away from home?
Why don't we go see what being home is really like?
The peacefulness, the serenity, the love, the laughter.
How could we resist such a beautiful place?
We shall never rest till we reach home.

WE

We all live surrounded by minds,
Exchanging ideas and relating finds.
We speak of thoughts and what we see,
But we don't realize the intensity of we.
Each person in their own domain
Of talk intense, we do refrain.
Let's go beyond the weather and sports,
And join our minds in ways of sorts.
Maybe what you're thinking I've already done,
And realizing this, we now are one.
We have a common point from whence to start,
And nothing outside may pull us apart.
We can pull together as a pair,
And come closer to our dream so rare.
For if another has an idea to share,
Invite him in without despair.
It may be that piece to our ongoing dream.
We're not only we were now a team.

Moving Experiences

A very special place once fully occupied,
Now an empty shell, stripped and pushed aside.
The whispering of the wind, pacing side to side,
Realization of the occupancy that doth no longer abide.
But yet a new place, an opening to be filled,
A new frontier, grounds yet to be tilled.
Exciting new plans to make this place unique,
Ideas steadily abounding, too much, so to speak.
This here, that there, to utilize the spaces,
What a change of pace to see no familiar faces.
Such a sudden shock, is it possible to succeed?
Almost as a prisoner who, after years, is freed.
A challenge in one way, an achievement in another,
Suddenly, a certain urgency for more grounds to discover.
Another special place once fully occupied,
Now an empty shell, stripped and pushed aside.

INFLUENTIAL CROSSINGS

From opposing points, we begin our direction,
Yet, at some given time, we make a connection.
This could be our only chance to possibly plant a seed,
Yet, each drawing on only what we need.
It's not our job to fertilize the terrain,
Nor are we capable of producing any rain.
Our job is only to throw out the seed,
Once this transpires, from this task, we're freed.
Onward we go to approach a new crossroad,
Our message staying with us as a heavy load.
There are many messages to be tossed to the ground,
But only the true messages will endure and abound.

Eyes Close the Mind

We know our needs deep inside,
Things of importance we choose to hide.
Not accidentally but purposely,
To enable ourselves to be as we see.
For if we didn't see would we care,
Or go with our needs without despair.
Open your eyes, close your mind,
If you choose to suffer in the happiness you find.
Or close your eyes, and open your mind,
And fulfill your needs till your hearts divine.
Never again will you feel left behind,
If you don't let the I's close the mind.

EQUALITY

If we were as unmolded clay,
our simple abilities would be the way.
We would not go by looks or show,
But what we retain and what we know.
No one could possibly say, "Hey, unfair,"
We would be all alike, and quite aware.
In choosing who is right for a job,
We would have to look carefully at the mob.
No exterior trait could we prefer,
not even the idea of him or her.
Is this what we need to make the world fair?
To overlook our traits as if they weren't there.
Is this wrong? I don't have to say,
But I choose to think, we'll get it one day.

JOINT IMPACT

Separated for years from interpretation of words,
divided by tradition, like different species of birds.
Soaring in one direction, our future is assured,
If you're not part of this flock, your just another bird.
Confrontations always, a test should colors fade,
In the midst of confrontation, our weakness has been made.
Realizing we've won a battle, we proudly stand and roar,
lowering our defenses, we forget were in a war.
We must realize the war is not with other birds,
It's the pioneer's opinions of misinterpreted words.
Powers and principalities and things unseen,
In numbers, we stand; and on God's word, we should lean.
A bird is a bird, a feather is a feather,
We must think this way to withstand the weather.
The weather is getting worse, we're being pushed back,
Our survival hinges on joint impact.

HONOR IN THE HIGHEST DEGREE

A challenge made known
to be conquered all alone,
prepared for battle
and sent out on your own.

What a proud feeling
in battle to stand,
facing the enemy
in a foreign land.

Not looking to slaughter,
not accepting defeat,
but opening the eyes
to ongoing deceit.

Not screaming or yelling,
not raising your voice,
but softly whispering,
"You do have a choice."

Scratching the surface
and planting the seed,
allowing the oppressed
from your knowledge to feed.

If but one soul
could be set free,
this would be honor
in the highest degree.

SEA WORTHY

The tide is rising; times are rough.
The boat is shifting; steering is tough.
Don't bail out, hold the ship.
If we don't panic, the boat won't tip.
Don't get flustered and feel lost,
You'll lose sight of where you're tossed.
Batten down the hatches, sound the alarm.
Do all you can to avoid the harm.
Keep a cool head, stand your ground,
Very soon, a solution will be found.

OFFSPRING

Such a beautiful tree to behold,
As beautiful to the eye as refined gold.
Silk leaves dangle, suspended above the ground,
shading everything that might be around.
Hardened bark to protect from foes,
deeply rooted to ward off woes.
A shelter to all who care to nest,
an uncomfortable place that allows no rest.
The fruit of the tree is rotten to the core,
The beauty of it acts only to lure.
It destroys all it envelopes, and whatever is around,
Destruction is even passed by falling seeds to the ground.
More corrupt fruit, more corrupt seed,
Like bacteria that has begun to feed.
The only chance the tree to uproot,
A new tree to plant that brings forth good fruit.

CHOICES

In our lives, we have to choose,
At times we win, at times we lose.
Sometimes, we overlook the right choice
because another's opinion has been voiced.
Should we choose the road that's hard,
Or take it easy and drop our guard?
The easy road is oh so appealing,
and the hard just gives an awful feeling.
No matter which road we choose to take,
A wiser person it shall make.
Don't go by the opinions of your peers.
Don't go on thoughts of other's tears.
Make the choice that you want most,
and about this choice, please don't boast.
For if you should, choose the wrong way,
You'll eat your words from day to day.
There is one thing that always stands true,
Eventually, true love will see you through.

DREAMS

In this world, we all have dreams,
Visions easy to touch, and so close it seems.
So we imagine ourselves as we see
in hopes to make it history.
We get distraught along the way
because we want it to happen today.
Then we see another day pass,
We find we're not moving quite so fast.
All of a sudden, we get depressed
because we can't put this dream to rest.
We poke and jab in an endless way,
only to find our path astray.
We stop to think where we went wrong,
to secure the path allowing us to move on.
When we finally reach our sacred ground,
It seems like a nothingness we have found.
We then envision another dream,
A little bit better, in some extreme.
Can we ever be happy and feel we're set?
Not as long as there are dreams, I'd surely bet.

PEEKING OUT

A test set forth with standards to meet,
no middle ground, victory, or defeat.
Eyes wide open to gauge the snares,
truly prepared for the task to bear.
Stepping out proudly, not sure where to start,
going on faith and assuming the part.
Hot coals on the ground, darts in the air,
so easy to avoid, seems almost unfair.
Only steps ahead, reaching out to touch
the ultimate victory that means so much.
A fly flitters by, and you pull back to swat,
in a moments time, your goal you've forgot.
The ground opens up, you fall in a rut,
your focus is scattered, your attention cut.
This test you must pass in order to grow,
embrace your friend, and you'll know your foe.

IN THE HEAT OF THE DAY

I dug a hole in the heat of the day,
Made fertile the soil, in which my toil lay.
I removed the tares that might cause delay,
I dug a hole in the heat of the day.
Seeds I threw into my perfect piece of turf,
The same seeds that will someday dress the earth.
My hole I covered with dark rich dirt,
To protect my seeds from any type of hurt.
I watched my efforts as days passed by,
Awaiting the growth that would appease my eye.
I re-dug the hole to see some progress,
But all my seeds were gone, much to my distress.
It probably was the birds that stole my seeds away,
Or possibly a storm that scattered them astray.
I had hoped others would not see me this way,
Hurt and angry, with doubt in my way.
In my moment of fury, with much silent rage,
I witnessed a beautiful thing in my age.
In spite of the fact that I dug up the ground,
there lay a sprout that had not been drown.
I pulled myself together and smiled through my frown,
and noticed many sprouts as I looked around.
Yes, I dug a hole in the heat of the day,
But God made fertile the soil, in which my toil lay.
He removed the tares that might stand in the way,
God blessed me to dig a hole in the heat of the day.

AGED

Let's see, what shall I do today? Go for a walk, work in the garden?
Maybe something exciting, like going fishing.
I don't know.
I'm feeling kind of tired.
My bones aren't as strong as they once
were, and my muscles are sore.
I think I'll just watch television for a while.
Well, maybe not, the picture on my new television is a tad blurry.
My hair, what little I have, is covered with white
paint; I tried to wash it but no luck.
Wait a minute; this is a brand-new method of cleaning my teeth.
Okay, now what was it I was about to do?
Well, since someone left the television on,
I suppose I'll watch it for a while.
Gee! The pictures on these new sets sure are blurry.

FALL

A nip in the air, a drop in degrees,
a spectrum of colors, a falling of leaves.
The final harvest, a sparseness of crop,
storage overflowing, but no time to stop.
An influx of competition in the same game,
the ultimate goal: to erase your name.
No grass to be cut, nor work to be done,
winterize the house and say bye to the sun.
Get oil in the lamps, and chop all the wood,
when the cold comes, you'll be in for good.
Hibernate for a season, no care to be found,
this season will end when you hear a great sound.

HANGING IN THERE

My head is low,
my spirit is broken.
I have no hope,
my dreams unspoken.
In front of many eyes,
I fade away,
a broken vessel,
in pieces I lay.
No will to think,
no tears left to cry,
drowning out my sorrows,
my tear ducts are dry.
A skeleton of a person
being covered with dust,
voices ringing by me,
make life seem unjust.
With one nostril exposed,
I turn in my grave,
a last blast of breath,
a longing wave.

NIGHT

A beautiful blanket of tinted blue,
rapidly, yet solemnly, changing hues.

From a lively brightness with plenty of life,
to a silent thick darkness, you could cut with a knife.

The air has become cool; the winds are at rest,
the bright glowing bulbs become welcome guests.

All birds are silent and few to be found,
except a circling bat that shadows the ground.

A stray dog breaks the silence once in a while,
with a small whimper or lonely howl.

Millions of diamonds scattered in the sky,
only to be touched by a curious eye.

Amongst the darkness, a reflecting balloon,
a friend in the dark, known as the moon.

Once this picture flourishes, which we happily invite,
It becomes our acquaintance, well known as night.

A PROPER WALK

If it's a blessing, give God thanks.
If it's a trial, give God thanks.
If you're feeling great, give God thanks.
If you're feeling down, give God thanks.
When you have victory, give God thanks.
When you taste defeat, give God thanks.
When you feel joy, give God thanks.
When you feel anger, give God thanks.
In everything, give God thanks.

DEATH

Finally, I made it home.
Home, the final resting place in the cold dark silence of the earth.
No more worries, no more bills, no longer shall
anything other than the walk I've made
through this wretched wilderness jab at me again.
My bed has been made.
All that I have encountered shall be with me for the duration.
As I look up from my paltry resting place, I
see the pathetic mess I've left behind.
Oh, how moving those looking down on me appear to be.
Why must they keep dropping these huge,
sorrowful, salty, despicable tears upon me?
Oh, tears so piercing to the soul.
Why is it that you waited till now to come my way?
Why could I not see you when my hands could
have come forward to wipe you away?
Either side I turn, I see woe and pity, pity and
woe, much lamenting and mournful souls.
The soil covering me probably feels like the base of
a thousand souls has crumbled on the spot.
These were the same who accused me, lied on me, and let me fall.
The ones I, myself, didn't treat as I would
have wanted to have been treated.
If there only was a chance to change these things.
Too late, too late!
Much too late!
Although I'm home, I may never rest.

Re-Birth

As the clouds scroll open to reveal the sky,
I gaze at the beauty with a longing eye.

Realizing my life that seemed so vast,
Was a mere spec of time now in the past.

I overcame the test, I trod through the storm.
I have no regrets my memories are warm.

Holding to my beliefs I receive my reward
With no inhibitions I run to my lord.

After all the predicaments that made my life seem hard
I can finally relax and drop my guard.

The beauty before me I cannot express
My soul is at ease, my mind at rest.

As you cry for me, I'm crying for you
Hoping you realize you can be here too.

I'm spending eternity in heavenly bliss,
Find your way here, this place don't miss.

ABOUT THE AUTHOR

Samuel L. Gregory Jr. has a unique gifting of God to discern the intricacies of an observation and bring out the hidden truths of a given situation. This gifting would allow Samuel to grasp an understanding of a given scenario, verbalize the impact, and communicate what others may have been thinking, or feeling, in a somewhat comedic nature.

As a young child, Samuel did not fully understand the gifting; however, it would surface in him, finding humor in every aspect of life, including hard times and hurtful situations. This humor, in many cases, was a salve which helped people to laugh when they were on the verge of tears.

Samuel, now in the role of a pastor, understands that this gifting of God has been given to aide him in healing individual's emotional state of being and helping them deal with the highs and lows of life. He also has found, in his later years, that this gifting was not only a discernment but, in many cases, God speaking hope and life through him.

In John 10:10, Jesus says, "The thief cometh not, but for to steal, and to kill, and to destroy: I am come that they might have life, and that they might have *it* more abundantly."

CPSIA information can be obtained
at www.ICGtesting.com
Printed in the USA
LVHW020923210221
679521LV00005B/721

9 781647 013271